Getting To Know...

Nature's Children

BIGHORN SHEEP

Bill Ivy

GROLIER
BOOKS

Facts in Brief

Classification of the Bighorn Sheep

Class: *Mammalia* (mammals)

Order: *Artiodactyla* (cloven-hoofed mammals)

Family: *Bovidae* (antelope, cattle, sheep, and goats)

Genus: *Ovis* (sheep)

Species: *Ovis canadensis*

World distribution. Exclusive to North America.

Habitat. Mountain slopes and foothills.

Distinctive physical characteristics. Large curving horns, spiralling in the male; short tail; coat is brown on the back, lighter on the underside.

Habits. Lives in bands of 10 to 100 animals; will fraternize with deer, domestic sheep, and Mountain Goats; is active in the daytime; migrates annually.

Diet. Grasses, shrubs, and lichens, and the twigs and needles of some trees.

Edited by: Elizabeth Grace Zuraw
Design/Photo Editor: Nancy Norton
Photo Rights: Ivy Images

ISBN: 0-7172-8836-6

Have you ever wondered . . .

Can you imagine what it would be like to climb the Rocky Mountains? You'd need ropes and picks and special shoes, and the venture would take you many, many days.

Mountain climbing is hard work for people—but not for Bighorn Sheep. The Bighorn is a natural athlete and can move with ease through mountainous areas that would quickly tire even the strongest two-legged athletes. No wonder the Bighorn is sometimes called "King of the Mountain."

You may think that all sheep are much the same—that they're all timid and meek and that they lead rather boring and unadventurous lives. If you do, you have some big surprises in store for you as you learn more about the Bighorn.

Bighorn Sheep, once numbering more than a million in North America, were as abundant in the mountains as buffalo were on the plains. Today fewer than 75,000 Bighorn remain.

Fun and Games

Young Bighorn Sheep, called *lambs,* like playing almost as much as you do. They even play some of the same games!

One of their favorites is "follow the leader." The lambs race nimbly after each other, without even seeming to notice that they're playing on the steep and craggy side of a mountain!

Another favorite game is "king of the castle." One lamb climbs to the top of a rock pile and dares the others to knock it off. Whichever lamb does so becomes the new king. This game is a lot of fun, but it's also good practice for the lambs. It teaches them rock-climbing, a mighty important survival skill for Bighorn Sheep.

Even at the age of two or three weeks, Bighorn lambs can jump and climb easily in rugged and dangerous mountain areas.

Bighorn Country

Bighorn Sheep are found in the western mountain regions of North America. Although their range extends south to Mexico, most make their home in the Rocky Mountains of Canada's Alberta and British Columbia. Bighorns prefer to live in wilderness areas, well away from people. They spend their summers high up in the mountains. Then, when the winter snows begin, they *migrate,* or move, down into the warmer valleys.

Opposite page: *Flexible, cushiony pads on their feet make it easy for Bighorns to grip the steep mountain terrain where they make their home.*

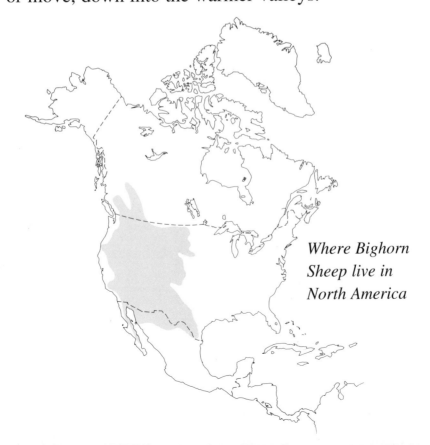

Where Bighorn Sheep live in North America

9

All in the Family

The Bighorn is closely related to farm sheep, and it also has several wild sheep cousins. Some of its wild relatives live in Asia and northern Russia, while others are found right here in North America. The Bighorn's closest wild cousin is the Dall's Sheep. It lives in the Yukon and Alaska.

The wild sheep that were the Bighorn's ancestors first came to North America more than 10,000 years ago. They migrated from Asia across a strip of land connecting Siberia to Alaska.

The Bighorn Up Close

At first glance it's hard to believe that the Bighorn is really a sheep at all. Its beautiful brown and white coat doesn't even look like wool! But the wool is there, hidden under a covering of *guard hairs,* long, coarse hairs that make up the outer layer of the Bighorn's coat. The guard hairs shed water and snow. Underneath the guard hairs is a layer of wool that traps body-warmed air close to the Bighorn's skin. The Bighorn's lower belly, rump, and muzzle tip are all creamy white. Its short tail is dark.

A full-grown male, or *ram,* may stand 3.3 feet (1 meter) tall at the shoulder and weigh as much as 340 pounds (155 kilograms). That's almost one and a half times bigger than farm sheep! The females, or *ewes,* are much smaller.

Notice how short and slender the ewe's horns are compared to the ram's thick and curving ones.

Super Senses

Both rams and ewes have excellent eyesight. Their large, amber-yellow eyes can spot something 1 mile (1.6 kilometers) away. If you wanted to see that far, you'd have to look through a pair of binoculars! When you consider that the Bighorn's sense of smell and hearing are almost as sharp as its eyesight, you can understand why it's nearly impossible to sneak up on one of these animals.

A Bighorn's sharp eyesight is its best defense against approaching intruders. A hungry enemy can be spotted long before it has a chance to start closing in on a Bighorn.

Watch out!

For part of the year, when they're high up in the mountains, full-grown Bighorns have few enemies. Only the cougar hunts there. The lambs, however, must be protected from Golden Eagles. These birds are large enough to swoop down from the sky and easily snatch a lamb. If a lamb senses danger from above, it scurries under its mother's belly, and she fends off the eagle with her horns.

During the winter, on the other hand, when Bighorn Sheep are down in the mountain valleys, even the full-grown adults need to be cautious. They must watch out for hungry wolves, bears, coyotes, bobcats, and lynx.

But catching a Bighorn isn't easy! This animal's keen senses give it plenty of advance warning of danger. Few predators are sure-footed enough to chase a Bighorn along narrow mountain trails. A *predator* is an animal that lives by hunting other animals. If a Bighorn can't outrun its enemy, it may turn and charge. Most predators would rather flee than confront a charging Bighorn.

Opposite page: *The safest place for little lambs is by their mother's side.*

17

Grass-loving Grazers

Bighorns, like people, have three main meal-
times each day—morning, midday, and late
afternoon. But unlike humans, this animal is
an *herbivore*—it eats only plants, not meat.
The Bighorn begins breakfast as soon as the
first rays of light appear. Its menu is simple
and almost always the same: grass, grass, and
more grass! Bluegrass, Junegrass, needlegrass,
and wheatgrass are some of its favorites. For
variety, it eats some other plants and shrubs,
such as wild rose, lupines, vetch, chokeberry,
horsetail, and willow.

In the winter when food is scarce, the
Bighorn eats less nutritious twigs and buds,
and even some evergreens, such as Douglas
Fir. It also digs beneath the snow with its feet
to get at whatever grass it can find.

*A mountain meadow is a popular
Bighorn luncheon spot.*

Eat Now, Chew Later

The Bighorn doesn't take a mouthful of food and chew it thoroughly before swallowing the way you do. Instead it swallows grass almost whole as it grazes. This unchewed food, called *cud,* goes into a special storage stomach. Later, when the Bighorn is relaxing, it brings this food back up into its mouth and chews it. This process is known as chewing the cud. You may have seen cows do the same thing.

After the cud has been chewed and swallowed again, the rest of the stomach finishes digesting it. Talk about stretching out a meal!

Various types of grasses make up most of the Bighorn's diet.

Opposite page:
Skillful jumpers with no fear of heights, Bighorns have been observed leaping from a 150-foot (46-meter) cliff, and landing perfectly!

Nimble Feet

The Bighorn is as agile on its feet as any circus performer. This animal can run fearlessly up and down steep mountain slopes and can balance on the narrowest of ledges. If you were to try to walk on the same icy and slippery rocks as the Bighorn does, in no time you'd be sliding down the mountain on the seat of your pants!

How does the Bighorn manage such feats? The secret is in the design of its feet, called *hoofs.* The outer edge of each hoof is hard and sharp for cutting into earth, gravel, and ice. The center is filled with a spongy material that provides traction. In addition, the Bighorn's split hoofs can pinch and hold onto rocks. Two smaller claws higher up on the foot serve as brakes should the Bighorn start to slide.

The Bighorn is famous for its jumping ability. It can leap 7 feet (2 meters) into the air! That ability comes in handy when it has to jump across a wide *crevice,* or gap in rock or ice. And if a ridge should start to break under its weight, the Bighorn can turn in midair and even land on its feet, just like a cat.

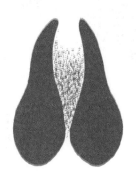

Bighorn hoof print

Bighorns' Big Horns

It's certainly no mystery how the Bighorn got its name! Few animals can boast of such impressive horns. The male's horns curl and often form a complete circle on each side of the head. This massive headset may weigh up to 30 pounds (14 kilograms) and measure 45 inches (114 centimeters) around the curve.

Although these big horns are handsome, they can cause problems. Not only are they heavy to carry, but sometimes a ram has difficulty seeing around them. Rams often rub their horns against rocks to wear them down.

Among horned animals, often only the males have horns. But this isn't the case in the Bighorn family. The females also have horns, although theirs are much smaller than the rams'. And instead of curling around in a circle, the females' curve only slightly.

A Bighorn never sheds its horns, which grow larger every year.

Opposite page: Scientists can tell a ram's age by counting the rings on its horns. Each section of rings shows a year's growth. A female's rings, however, don't accurately reflect her age.

Snorts and Baas

If you could listen in on some Bighorns "talking," you might think you were in a barn-yard. They sound just like their cousins, the farm sheep.

A low-pitched baa is a mother's way of calling a lamb to her. It means danger may be nearby. Lambs *bleat,* or give a whining cry, to let their mothers know they're hungry or tired. But adult male Bighorn seldom "talk." Instead they snort, usually to let other males know they're ready for a fight.

Like most young animals, Bighorn lambs are curious about everything and eager to explore their surroundings.

Leader of the Pack

Bighorns live in *bands,* or groups, numbering from 10 to 100 sheep. During the summer, the males form their own "bachelor clubs" of about 10 rams. These male bands have a leader, often the sheep with the biggest horns. This is because large horns usually mean that their owner is healthy. Size and strength make such a ram a natural leader, but sometimes, other rams challenge his leadership by butting at his horns.

At the same time, the females and young sheep form bands of their own. Away from the males, they graze leisurely on the mountain meadows. An older, experienced ewe takes charge of the band and stands guard as the other sheep feed. At the first sign of danger, she sounds an alarm by stamping a foot. Then she bolts away, leading the fleeing band to safety higher up the mountainside.

Come winter, the rams, ewes, and young join together, forming larger bands. They don't separate into smaller groups again until the following spring.

Opposite page: *Members of a male band share a grassy slope. Bighorns avoid forests unless they find themselves cornered by an enemy, with no nearby cliff to escape to.*

Down from the High Country

Winters are harsh in the mountains. A Bighorn prepares for bad weather by eating as much as it can to store up a thick layer of fat.

After the first heavy snowfall, the band begins its journey from the high country to the more sheltered valleys below. The same routes are used year after year. Bighorns may travel 25 miles (40 kilometers) or more before finally reaching their destination.

Bighorns travel in single file, following their leader. When sheep in the band try to pass the lead ram, he uses his horns to keep them in line. Even though a single Bighorn can run as fast as 35 miles (56 kilometers) per hour, the band seldom travels faster than a trot. Bighorns are good swimmers and often cross rivers and lakes along the way. From time to time the band rests. When they sleep, Bighorns fold their legs under their bodies to keep warm.

A Bighorn's thick, fleecy coat provides cozy protection against winter's cold weather.

Hard Times

For a winter home, the band chooses a south-facing slope that is kept fairly clear of snow by the sun and wind. Finding enough to eat in winter is often a problem. Should the snow become too deep to paw through, many Bighorns may go hungry. And sometimes, what snow there is may be the main or only source of drinking water. During a bad storm, Bighorns often huddle together against a cliff or take shelter in a cave. Like so many of us, they eagerly await the arrival of spring.

Heavy snowfalls may make it difficult for Bighorns to get the food they need.

The Challenge

During November and December, once the Bighorns are down in the valleys, a great deal of fighting takes place among the rams. It's *mating season,* the time of year during which animals come together to produce young. If two males choose the same female, they will fight to see who wins her. Their main weapon is their mighty horns.

First the two challengers size each other up. They lower their heads to show off their enormous horns. Then, snorting and grunting, they begin to push and shove each other. Sometimes one of the rams may kick. If one of them doesn't back down at that point, they prepare for a real "head to head" battle.

Overleaf:
*Ewes rest quietly
while rams
compete for mates.*

*"Getting pushy" is usually the first
step in a fight between two rams.*

Head to Head

The Bighorn rams circle each other at a distance of about 30 feet (9 meters). As if on signal, they rear up on their hind legs. Then they charge, heads down, at full speed. The impact of head crashing into head sends ripples through their bodies, and the echoing crack can often be heard as far as a mile (1.6 kilometers) away!

Slightly stunned by the blow, the groggy fighters shake their heads. When the dizziness clears, they back off for another charge. Again and again they butt each other until one of them has had enough. This may take hours. Incredibly, very few Bighorns are ever seriously hurt, though horns often break or crack, and occasionally a Bighorn ends up with a broken nose or knocked out cold! But basically, their double-layered skulls, massive neck muscles, and thick facial hide absorb most of the force of the blows.

Head-butting duels can break out at any time of year as rams often test each other's might. And fights can go on and on. A scientist once observed two rams colliding about 5 times an hour for 25 hours straight!

New Coats

One nice thing about spring is that you no longer have to wear your heavy winter clothes. Neither do Bighorns. Once warmer weather reaches the mountains, Bighorns *molt,* or shed their thick winter coats. The coats lighten in color and gradually thin out. At this stage the sheep look rather shaggy with long, matted strands of their old coats hanging from their bodies. To help loosen and shed this unwanted hair, Bighorns rub themselves against rocks and trees.

A Bighorn's lightweight spring coat will start to thicken again in the fall—just in time for winter.

By midsummer, this Bighorn will be nearly bare-skinned, but by fall, it'll be growing a thick new coat.

Mountain Nursery

Opposite page:
A Bighorn lamb weighs only about 8 pounds at birth. If it's a twin, it may weigh a little less. But baby Bighorns grow very quickly.

While the Bighorns are still in the valleys, the lambs are born. A mother Bighorn leaves the herd in search of a sheltered nursery, probably a steep rock cliff or a high ledge. Usually only one lamb is born, but sometimes a mother may have twins.

As soon as she's given birth, the ewe licks her baby's wet, woolly, light brown coat until it's dry. Then mother and baby gently touch noses to learn each other's scent.

The trembling youngster struggles to its feet and balances on wobbly legs. Only 16 inches (40 centimeters) tall, the newborn already has tiny buttons on its head where its horns will grow.

As soon as it's standing, the lamb cuddles under its mother's belly and begins to *nurse,* or drink milk from its mother's body. The proud mother baas softly to her baby, who grows stronger every minute on the diet of its mother's rich milk.

Even the most frolicsome youngster needs a rest now and then, especially on the long trek up the mountain.

The Long Climb

Newborn lambs receive a friendly welcome when they join the rest of the band. Many year-old Bighorns and single females crowd around the newest members of the group. Sometimes a new mother and her baby need to sneak away from the flock to nurse in peace!

Most human babies are about a year old before they take their first steps on their own. But Bighorn babies can walk when they are only a few hours old. And they can run and jump within a few days!

Growing up quickly is important for a Bighorn lamb. When it's only a few weeks old, it must join the rest of the band as it travels up the mountain to its summer meadows.

This is a long hard climb for a baby lamb. It stays close to its mother for protection and food.

Part of the Flock

Summer is a good time for a Bighorn lamb. There's plenty of food on the mountain meadows, and bit by bit the youngster stops nursing and starts eating grass like its mother. All that food makes the lamb strong and frisky. It's soon racing around and playing games with the other Bighorns its own age. While the youngsters are having their fun, the mothers often take turns babysitting.

By the end of their first summer, the lambs weigh about 75 pounds (34 kilograms). And by the time the Bighorns are ready for their journey down the mountain to their winter home, the lambs no longer need to stay close to their mothers. They're part of the flock now, and will soon begin to raise families of their own. When a young female is two years old, she's ready to start a family. Males mature at about four years of age.

If a Bighorn practices its survival skills well and is lucky, it can enjoy an average life span of about 10 years. Some even live to an age of about 20 years.

Words To Know

Band A group of Bighorn Sheep.

Bleat A lamb's whining cry.

Crevice A gap in rock or ice.

Cud Hastily swallowed food brought back up for chewing by cud-chewing animals such as sheep, deer, and cows.

Ewe A female sheep.

Guard hairs Long coarse hairs that make up the outer layer of a Bighorn's coat.

Herbivore An animal that eats only plants.

Hoofs The feet of sheep, deer, and some other animals.

Horn Outgrowth on the heads of sheep, cattle, and some other animals. Horns do not fall off every year, as do antlers, the type of growths found on members of the deer family.

Lamb A young sheep.

Mating season The time of year during which animals come together to produce young.

Migration The move some animals make from one place to another to find food, a suitable climate to live, or a place to mate and raise young.

Molt To shed one coat of fur or feathers and grow another.

Nurse To drink milk from the mother's body.

Plains Flat, grassy, treeless areas of land.

Predator An animal that lives by hunting other animals.

Ram A male sheep.

Index

PHOTO CREDITS
Cover: Wayne Lankinen, *Valan Photos.* **Interiors:** *Valan Photos:* Stephen J. Krasemann, 4; Wayne Lankinen, 7, Thomas Kitchin, 15, 20-21; J. D. Markou, 16; Esther Schmidt, 23, 32; Hälle Flygare, 24; Dennis Schmidt, 31. /*Ivy Images:* Alan & Sandy Carey, 8, 43; Don Johnston, 12, 44; Robert McCaw, 34, 36-37. /Wayne Lankinen, 11, 19. /Tim Fitzharris, 26, 40. /Len Rue, Jr., 28. /Duane Sept, 39.

Getting To Know...

Nature's Children

PRAIRIE DOGS

Celia B. Lottridge
and
Susan Horner

GROLIER
BOOKS

Facts in Brief

Classification of the Prairie Dog

    Class: *Mammalia* (mammals)

    Order: *Rodentia* (rodents)

    Family: *Sciuridae* (squirrel family)

    Genus: *Cynomys*

    Species: *Cynomys ludovicianus* (includes 5 subspecies)

World distribution. Exclusive to North America.

Habitat. Open grassy plains.

Distinctive physical characteristics. Brownish fur, lighter underside; short tail and ears; color of tail varies with subspecies.

Habits. Lives in large close-knit communities; active only during the day; individuals greet each other by touching muzzles or "kissing."

Diet. Leaves, roots, weeds, and grasses.

Edited by: Elizabeth Grace Zuraw
Design/Photo Editor: Nancy Norton
Photo Rights: Ivy Images

ISBN: 0-7172-8837-4

Have you ever wondered . . .

Some wild animals live alone, some live with a mate, and some live in family groups. But there is one kind of animal that lives with hundreds of others in an area known as a town. This animal is the Prairie Dog, and the place where it lives is called a Prairie Dog town.

Imagine you're visiting such a town early on a summer morning. The first thing you'd see is a *prairie*—a flat, grassy expanse of land—dotted with low mounds of dirt. A look at one of the mounds would reveal a hole— the entrance to a Prairie Dog's home.

If you watched this entrance carefully you might spot a Prairie Dog's small tan head poke up out of it. But one move from you and the Prairie Dog would disappear back down the hole. It might pop up again, though, if you waited very quietly, and it might even come all the way out for a longer look around.

Let's find out more about these fascinating little town-dwellers.

Resembling a deserted, bumpy landscape, a Prairie Dog town can reach as far as the eye can see.

Rise and Shine

When the Prairie Dog comes out of its *den,* or home, you can see that it's about the size of a little puppy. Not including its tail, it's about 12 inches (30 centimeters) long and is covered with thick tan and brown fur. Its body is pudgy, and its short tail—4 inches (10 centimeters) long—sticks out behind.

If the Prairie Dog sees nothing threatening, it tilts back its head and makes a few short sharp sounds. With each loud chirp, its tail quivers and seems to signal "all clear!"

Soon more Prairie Dogs come out of their homes. They nuzzle and greet each other with touches that look like kisses. When morning greetings are over, the business of the day begins. The Prairie Dogs feed busily, bask in the sun, take dust baths, visit neighbors, and wash themselves. A new day is underway in the Prairie Dog town.

When first leaving its home in the morning, a Prairie Dog sometimes stands atop its mound for as long as half an hour. That way, it can check to be really sure it's safe outside.

Are Prairie Dogs Really Dogs?

There are five kinds of Prairie Dogs in North America. The most common are the Black-tailed and White-tailed Prairie Dogs. Except for the color of their tails, they look very much alike.

The Black-tailed Prairie Dog is found on the flat prairies from southern Saskatchewan in Canada to Oklahoma and Texas. The White-tailed Prairie Dog lives farther west, in the treeless foothills of Colorado, Utah, and New Mexico.

Because their alarm call sounds like the bark of a small dog, early prairie settlers called these animals Prairie Dogs or Prairie Barkers. But Prairie Dogs aren't really dogs. They're *rodents,* animals with a certain kind of teeth that are especially good for gnawing. Prairie Dogs' teeth can easily bite through tough roots and stalks.

The Prairie Dog's rodent relatives include mice, chipmunks, beavers, and Ground Squirrels, to which it is most closely related.

Opposite page: *From the front, it's hard to know which kind of Prairie Dog you're looking at. But the tail will quickly tell you this is a Black-tailed.*

Prairie Dog Homes

The hole at the top of a Prairie Dog mound is the entrance to the Prairie Dog's *burrow,* or underground home. The entrance hall is a long tunnel 10 to 14 feet (3 to 4 meters) straight down. Then the tunnel levels off, continuing deep underground for up to 80 or more feet (24 or more meters). Halfway down the entrance tunnel is a shelf where the Prairie Dog can turn around or hide in case of danger.

Small side tunnels lead to sleeping rooms, toilets, storage rooms, and a larger room—a nursery—where the babies are born. The main tunnel often continues past the bedrooms, joining several burrows together. This way, neighbors can visit without going outside!

The burrow is warm in winter and cool in summer because it's so deep. And it stays dry because the entrance tunnel goes down steeply and then turns up again. That way, water cannot flow into the tunnels that lay beyond.

Cutaway of a Prairie Dog burrow

These Prairie Dogs are hard at work building up their mound. Prairie Dogs are noted for their cooperative efforts in building and maintaining their burrows.

Miniature Mountains

As Prairie Dogs dig their burrows, they push the loose earth out of the tunnel with their front legs and foreheads until there is a pile of dirt at the entrance. Then they scrape up more earth from around the edges of the pile to make the mound even bigger. Finally, they butt at the loose heap of dirt with their foreheads and noses until they've shaped it into a firm mound. If you looked carefully at a mound, you might even be able to see its owner's nose prints!

Prairie Dogs spend a lot of time on their mounds sunning and chatting with each other. Young Prairie Dogs play by climbing up and down these miniature mountains.

Their mounds are very important to Prairie Dogs. Because these structures are higher than the land around them, they make good lookout posts. By standing on their mounds and stretching as tall as possible, Prairie Dogs have a good view all around. The mound also serves as a dam to keep any runoff from rain showers from flowing into the burrow's entrance.

A Close-knit Community

Prairie Dogs live in groups called *coteries.*
A coterie may start with only one male and
one female, but it soon grows to include other
adults, some *yearlings,* or one-year-old
youngsters, and a number of babies. Some
coteries have as many as 35 members, but
most have fewer than a dozen.

A coterie builds as many burrows and
mounds as are needed to hold all of its
members. Digging the burrows and keeping
them in good repair is a big job, and all the
Prairie Dogs in the coterie help with the work.
They use their long front claws and short
strong legs for digging and their sharp teeth
for cutting through roots.

*The tan and brown fur of Prairie Dogs is almost
the same color as the dried earth around their
burrows. Blending in with their surroundings
helps protect these animals from enemies.*

A male leader noisily scolds an intruder to scare it off and sometimes even gives an unwelcome stranger a quick bite on the rump.

16

Top Dog

A coterie's *territory* consists of the mounds and burrows where the coterie lives. It also includes some of the surrounding land. Visitors are not welcome.

Each coterie is headed by the strongest male. He's the one who comes out of the hole first in the morning and goes in last at night. He knows exactly how much territory belongs to his coterie. If he finds a member of another coterie in his territory, he quickly chases the intruder away.

Overleaf:
The Prairie Dog's high-set eyes enable the animal to detect motion over distances as great as hundreds of yards (meters).

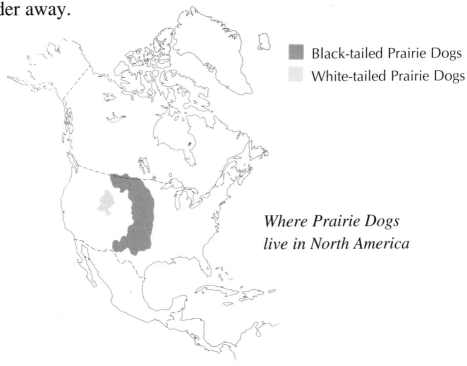

■ Black-tailed Prairie Dogs
■ White-tailed Prairie Dogs

Where Prairie Dogs live in North America

Prairie Dog Town

The territories of many coteries taken together form a Prairie Dog town. Prairie Dog towns, like the towns that people live in, may be large or small. One huge Prairie Dog town that existed in Texas many years ago held 400 million Prairie Dogs. It should have been called a Prairie Dog city!

Most Prairie Dog towns are much smaller than that. Usually they cover about 200 acres (81 hectares) and are home to about 140 coteries, or more than 1,000 Prairie Dogs.

And, like towns that people live in, Prairie Dog towns are divided into smaller units, a bit like our city blocks. These are called *wards* and are separated from each other by natural boundaries such as hills, trees, and different kinds of grass.

Prairie Dogs grow up to weigh as much as three pounds. Their life span is about five years.

Keeping Watch

Every adult Prairie Dog spends some time being a *sentinel,* or guard, that watches out for signs of danger. While the other Prairie Dogs sun themselves, eat, or play, the sentinel sits on its haunches on top of its mound and acts as lookout.

If a sentinel sees the shadow of a hawk, hears the yip of a coyote, or senses any unusual movement nearby, it rises up on its toes, flicks its tail, and barks loudly. Quick as a flash, all nearby Prairie Dogs—as well as the watchful sentinel—dive into their burrows for safety.

For a few moments, all is quiet. Then the sentinel pokes up its head. If the danger has passed, it makes an "all clear" whistling sound. As quickly as they had disappeared, all the Prairie Dogs begin popping out of their burrows to resume their busy day. But Prairie Dogs are noted for their patience. Sometimes they'll quietly stay in their burrows for even an hour until they hear a distinct all-clear bark.

Opposite Page:
At the first sign of danger, this alert sentinel will sound an alarm. Sometimes a group of four Prairie Dogs stands guard, one facing in each direction.

Who Goes There?

Prairie Dogs use touch and smell to recognize the members of their coterie. They know each other very well because they spend a lot of time stroking and *grooming,* or cleaning, each other with their paws. They often groom each other while they sun themselves. They also rub necks, touch noses, and "kiss" frequently while they're building mounds or looking for food.

Because they know the touch and smell of each other so well, they can easily tell friend from stranger. That's why Prairie Dogs greet each other with a touch that's like a kiss. That kiss lets each dog get a good sniff of the other.

Mother and baby greet each other by nuzzling and kissing.

What's for Dinner?

Prairie Dogs don't have to travel far to find food. They eat the grasses and other leafy plants that grow around their mounds. They choose their favorite foods by smell and nip the plants off neatly with their sharp teeth. Then they sit up, hold the stem or leaf in their front paws, and nibble away. The Prairie Dogs' grassy diet has a useful side effect: All the munching keeps the grass around their mounds well trimmed, giving them a good view over their territory.

Opposite page: *Like their relatives the squirrels, Prairie Dogs hold food in their front paws.*

Plants also provide Prairie Dogs with the water they need. The stalks of prickly thistles are especially juicy. Prairie Dogs are careful to bite the stalks close to the ground so that they don't get pricked.

In the summer, Prairie Dogs spend more than half of their waking hours eating. It's important for them to store up fat in their bodies while plants are green and plentiful. In winter, food will be hard to find, and the Prairie Dogs will have to live on the fat stored in their bodies.

Sun Worshippers

Prairie Dogs love warm sunny days. They spend their time waddling about their territory, eating, repairing their mounds, greeting each other with kisses, grooming each other, and keeping watch.

If it gets too hot in the middle of the day, they go into their burrows for a while. Rain, too, will drive them inside. But after a rain, they love to come out and eat. That's when the plants are especially moist and delicious.

Wind makes Prairie Dogs uneasy, probably because its sound covers up sounds that might warn them of approaching danger. On windy days Prairie Dogs are especially alert and quickly duck into their burrows at any unusual noise or movement.

Sometimes it's fun just to lounge about lazily in the sun and munch on a tasty snack.

A Cozy Retreat

As winter approaches, Prairie Dogs concentrate on eating so that they can store fat on their bodies. In cold weather, however, they slow down and spend most of their time inside their burrows. But unlike squirrels, they don't *hibernate,* or go into a kind of heavy wintertime sleep. When the weather warms up in winter, Prairie Dogs pop out for a look around and a quick snack on whatever food they can find. But when winter winds start blowing again, they retreat to the warmth of their underground homes.

Prairie Dogs line their bedrooms with dried grasses and weeds. This makes the burrow a comfy place to rest in.

Mating Time

In early spring, Prairie Dogs become lively again. Food is still hard to find, but they come out of their burrows to feel the warmth of the sunshine and to greet each other. Soon all the coteries in the town are out. The mounds are abuzz with activity as well as the yipping conversations of Prairie Dogs.

March and April is *mating season,* the time of year during which animals come together to produce young. Then both males and females clean out the old burrows and dig new tunnels. The adult females are careful to line the largest sleeping room in the burrow with soft, dry grass to make nests for the babies that soon will be born.

Although young Prairie Dogs are very curious, most of the time they stay close to home. When they're not resting, they love to play. The youngsters romp and somersault, play-fight, jump over one another, play tag, and do a lot of chirping and squealing.

*Pups must learn to be watchful of their surroundings.
A mound, which can be 1 or 2 feet (about 3 or 6
decimeters) high, offers a good vantage point for
observing the neighborhood.*

Prairie Dog Pups

The babies, called *pups,* are born in late May. There are usually four or five babies in a *litter,* the group of animals born together. The new pups are red, wrinkled, hairless, blind little creatures about 3 inches (about 8 centimeters) long from nose to tail.

A Prairie Dog mother looks after her babies carefully. For the first few weeks she doesn't allow anyone else near them. She starts to teach them how to groom by licking and rubbing them frequently.

The pups grow fast from *nursing,* or drinking the rich milk from their mother's body. In three weeks their fur has grown in. Now they can squeak and roll around a little.

At about five weeks, the pups open their eyes. They're starting to look a lot like their parents. Soon they're running around the burrow, trying to bark. It's not long until the great day when they come out of their burrows and tumble down their mounds into the great wide world.

Bringing Up the Babies

Once the pups have come out of their burrows, every Prairie Dog in the town helps raise and care for them. The little ones run from one burrow to another to play with the babies from the other litters. Sometimes they sleep over at another pup's home. Unlike adult Prairie Dogs, the youngsters are even allowed to visit other coteries.

Both male and female adults spend much time grooming the pups, kissing them, and playing tumbling and chasing games with them. The pups love these games so much that they sometimes become nuisances. An adult who is trying to keep watch or eat a meal sometimes has to discourage the youngsters with little nips or pushes.

The babies soon learn to dart into their burrows if anything seems strange or unusual. They pop in and out of the holes hundreds of times a day like furry little jack-in-the-boxes.

But their babyhood is short. At seven weeks of age, pups can find and eat food on the own. And at ten weeks, they're fully able to look after themselves.

Opposite page:
An adult greets a pup and keeps an eye on their surroundings. Prairie Dogs have a number of enemies to watch out for, including coyotes, bobcats, snakes, eagles, hawks, wolves, and badgers.

Overleaf:
This drawing is an artist's view of Prairie Dog pups huddling together in the nursery, their special room in the burrow.

37

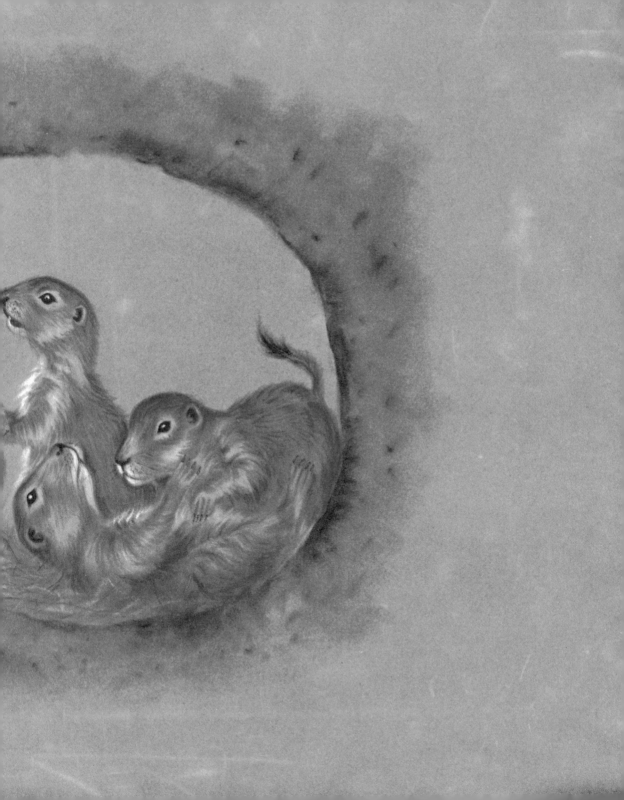

Learning To Be Prairie Dogs

Toward summer's end, the spring babies are nearly as big as their parents. Their playing has taught them how to recognize each other and how to groom and "talk" to each other.

Now they begin to learn about territories. They're no longer welcome in the territory of other coteries. They'll be driven back to their own area if they cross the boundary.

The youngsters love to imitate the older Prairie Dogs. By copying their behavior, the pups learn how to find food, respond to alarm calls, and give calls.

One call the young Prairie Dogs especially like is the territorial call, which says, "Here I am and here is my territory." To make the call, the Prairie Dog stands on its hind legs; thrusts out its front paws; raises its nose to the sky; and gives a loud two-note bark. The young ones practice this endlessly. Sometimes they get so excited that they lean too far back and end up tumbling backward over and over down the mound!

Opposite page: *Practice makes perfect. Getting on its hind legs and throwing its front paws out are the first steps in making a call.*

Growing Families

By late summer, young Prairie Dogs, like their elders, are spending most of their time eating to store fat for the winter. They'll spend the winter in the burrow where they were born. In the spring, they'll be yearlings. Then they'll welcome the new litters of babies in the coteries. By the time the young Prairie Dogs are two years old, they'll be ready to mate and have their own babies.

Prairie Dogs enjoy each other's company. These sociable little creatures have a wide variety of cousins all around the world, but they themselves are found only in North America.

Moving On

A coterie cannot keep growing forever or there wouldn't be enough food for all of its members. So every year some Prairie Dogs have to leave their coteries.

Yearling males sometimes go off to establish coteries of their own. Sometimes an adult male and female may go together and build new burrows and new mounds, leaving the younger members of their original coterie to carry on. Females sometimes leave to join other coteries.

New coteries, new mounds, and new burrows all become part of a Prairie Dog town where Prairie Dogs stand sentinel, work, and play together.

Prairie Dogs tend to be stay-at-homes. They travel only as far from their burrows as they have to when looking for food. Being home-bodies also insures safety. If need be, Prairie Dogs can quickly take cover from enemies.

Words To Know

Burrow   A hole in the ground dug by an animal to be used as a home.

Coterie   A group of Prairie Dogs made up of 8 to 35 members.

Den   An animal home.

Groom   To clean.

Hibernation   A kind of long, heavy sleep that some animals take in the winter, during which their breathing and heart rates slow, and their body temperature drops.

Litter   The group of animal brothers and sisters born together.

Mating season   The time of year during which animals come together to produce young.

Nursing   Drinking milk from a mother's body.

Prairie   A flat treeless area where grasses grow.

Pup   A young Prairie Dog.

Rodent   An animal with a certain kind of teeth that are especially good for gnawing.

Sentinel   A guard that watches for danger and signals alarm if necessary.

Territory   The area that an animal or group of animals lives in and often defends from other animals of the same kind.

Ward   A subdivision of a Prairie Dog town.

Yearling   An animal that is one year old.

Index

PHOTO CREDITS
Cover: Barry Ranford. **Interiors:** *Ivy Images:* Don Johnston, 4, 16, 34; Robert McCaw, 7. /*Valan Photos:* Stephen J. Krasemann, 8, 25, 33, 42-43; Esther Schmidt, 15, 21, 40; Wayne Lankinen, 18-19, 29, 30; Wilf Schurig, 22; Dennis Schmidt, 26, 46. /*Thomas Stack & Associates:* Dominique Braud, 12; /*Visuals Unlimited:* Carlyn Galati, 36; Milton H. Tierney Jr., 44.